TARDIGI

FEATURES, SIGNIFICANCE, ECOLOGY AND BEHAVIOUR OF THE WATER BEAR

BY MICHELLE D. TONY

Table of Contents

INTRODUCTION 3
CHAPTER ONE 4
   OVERVIEW OF TARDIGRADE 4
   ACTUAL QUALITIES 6
   RESILENCE AND METHODS FOR SURVIVING .. 8
CHAPTER TWO 10
   IMPORTANCE OF TARDIGRADE 10
   REDISCOVERY AND FORMAL NAMING 11
   TARDIGRADES IN SPACE 12
CHAPTER THREE 19
   MORPHOLOGY AND BODY DESIGN 19
   UNIQUE ADAPTATIONS AND FEATURES 23
CHAPTER FOUR 28
   REPRODUCTIVE SYSTEM 28
CHAPTER FIVE 33
   TERRESTIAL ENVIRONMENT 33
   AQUATIC ENVIRONMENT OF TARDIGRADE . 37
   EXTREMOPHILIC HABITAT 41
CHAPTER SIX 46
   TARDIGRADE ECOLOGY AND BEHAVIOR 46
   NOURISHING PROPENSITIES AND DIET 46

INTRODUCTION

Tardigrades are interesting animals they are likewise called water bears or greenery piglets. They are minute creatures that are viewed as from one side of the planet to the other

A tardigrade, is a minuscule creature that has a place with the phylum Tardigrada. These interesting animals are known for their capacity to endure outrageous circumstances. They can be tracked down in different living spaces, including greeneries, lichens, freshwater, and marine conditions.

CHAPTER ONE
OVERVIEW OF TARDIGRADE

Tardigrades are inconceivably strong and can get through conditions that would be destructive to most different life forms. They are fit for enduring outrageous temperatures, from as low as - 272 degrees Celsius (- 458 degrees Fahrenheit) to as high as 149 degrees Celsius (300 degrees Fahrenheit). They can likewise endure elevated degrees of radiation, outrageous tensions, and, surprisingly, the vacuum of room.

To endure such unforgiving circumstances, tardigrades enter a state called cryptobiosis, where they suspend their metabolic exercises. They can make due in this torpid state for a really long time and resume typical exercises once the circumstances become great once more.

Tardigrades have an extraordinary life systems with four sets of legs, each closure in hooks or pull cups. They likewise have a rounded mouthpart called a stylet, which they use to penetrate plant and creature cells to benefit from their items.

These surprising little animals have caught the interest of researchers and specialists because of their amazing flexibility and likely applications in different fields. Their capacity to get through outrageous circumstances has suggestions for space investigation, medication, and the investigation of life on The planet

Tardigrades, are minuscule, water-staying creatures having a place with the phylum Tardigrada. Regardless of their minor size, going from 0.1 to 1.5

millimeters, they show momentous versatility and flexibility, making them subjects of interest in logical examination

ACTUAL QUALITIES

• Tardigrades have an unmistakable barrel-molded body with four sets of thickset legs, each furnished with hooks or pull cups.

• Their bodies are commonly fragmented, and they might seem straightforward or clear.

• The presence of a fingernail skin gives insurance, and a few animal varieties display pigmentation

• Tardigrades can be tracked down in different natural surroundings, going from earthbound conditions like greeneries, lichens, soil, and leaf litter to oceanic conditions like freshwater and marine residue.

- They flourish in wet circumstances however can persevere through outrageous conditions, including deserts and polar districts

Taking care of and Multiplication

- Tardigrades are microphagous, benefiting from liquids removed from plant cells, green growth, and little spineless creatures.

- They replicate both physically and abiogenetically, with females equipped for laying eggs through parthenogenesis

RESILENCE AND METHODS FOR SURVIVING

- Tardigrades are eminent for their capacity to endure outrageous circumstances through a condition of cryptobiosis, where metabolic exercises stop, and water content reductions to approach zero.

- They can get through outrageous temperatures, tensions, radiation, and, surprisingly, the vacuum of room.

- Cryptobiosis permits them to endure drying up and continue ordinary exercises when rehydrated

Transformative HISTORY

- Tardigrades have a long transformative history, with fossils tracing all the way back to the Cambrian time frame quite a long time back.

- Their developmental transformations have empowered them to endure through different natural changes

CHAPTER TWO

IMPORTANCE OF TARDIGRADE

- Tardigrades are subjects of serious logical interest because of their outrageous flexibility and novel natural highlights.

- Analysts concentrate on them for bits of knowledge into endurance components, potential biotechnological applications, and their significance to astrobiology

- In spite of their versatility, tardigrades are helpless to territory misfortune and natural debasement.

- Preservation endeavors are significant to keeping up with biodiversity and figuring out the natural jobs of tardigrades

REDISCOVERY AND FORMAL NAMING

- Tardigrades acquired further consideration when a researcher and minister rediscovered and efficiently portrayed them in 1777. He begat the expression "Tardigrada," signifying "slow steppers," mirroring their stumbling development

- All through the nineteenth hundred years, researchers dug further into the characterization of tardigrades. They were perceived as an unmistakable phylum, Tardigrada, and endeavors were made to classify various species in view of morphological qualities

EARLY Examinations ON Life structures and PHYSIOLOGY Propels in microscopy permitted scientists to investigate the life systems and physiology of tardigrades more meticulously. Early examinations zeroed in on understanding their remarkable highlights, for example, the pawed legs and capacity to endure drying up

INNOVATIVE ADVANCES

- Propels in microscopy, hereditary qualities, and atomic science in the late twentieth 100 years and past have considered more top to bottom investigations of tardigrades. Specialists have investigated their hereditary qualities, advancement, and the instruments behind their flexibility.

TARDIGRADES IN SPACE

- Progresses in microscopy, hereditary qualities, and sub-atomic science in the late twentieth hundred years and past have considered more top to bottom investigations of tardigrades. Analysts have investigated their hereditary qualities, advancement, and the systems behind their versatility.

Proceeded with Investigation and Exploration

- Tardigrades keep on being a subject of continuous logical examination. Their exceptional elements and flexibility make them important for concentrates on in astrobiology, biotechnology, and figuring out the restrictions of life on The planet and then some

SIGNIFICANCE OF TARDIGRADES IN LOGICAL EXPLORATION

Tardigrades, otherwise called water bears or greenery piglets, hold huge significance in different logical disciplines because of their exceptional natural highlights and wonderful versatility. The regions where they cause significant commitments to incorporate

1. Extreme Versatility

- Tardigrades are prestigious for their capacity to get through outrageous circumstances, including drying up, outrageous temperatures, radiation, and the vacuum of room. Understanding the atomic and physiological systems behind their versatility can give bits of knowledge into the constraints of life on The planet and the potential for life in extraterrestrial conditions

2. Astrobiology

- Tardigrades are viewed as model creatures for astrobiology. Their capacity to endure cruel circumstances makes them applicable to the investigation of possible extraterrestrial life and the circumstances expected for life to exist on different planets or moons

3. Cryptobiosis and Anhydrobiosis

- The peculiarity of cryptobiosis, where tardigrades enter a condition of suspended movement, and anhydrobiosis, their capacity to endure outrageous drying out, are specifically noteworthy. Examination into these cycles could have applications in biotechnology, medication, and the safeguarding of organic materials

4. Biotechnological Applications

- Tardigrades' exceptional capacities might have functional applications in biotechnology. Understanding their pressure obstruction components could move advancements in fields like cryopreservation, where cells, tissues, or even organs are safeguarded at very low temperatures

5. Medicine and Human Wellbeing

- The investigation of tardigrades might offer bits of knowledge into stress obstruction at the cell level. This information could have suggestions for clinical exploration, possibly prompting the advancement of treatments that upgrade cell strength and advance results in circumstances of stress, for example, during organ transplantation

6. Environmental Checking

- Tardigrades are delicate to changes in their current circumstance, making them possible signs of ecological wellbeing. Observing tardigrade populaces in unambiguous biological systems could give early admonitions of ecological aggravations or contamination

7. Evolutionary Investigations

- Tardigrades have a long developmental history, going back more than 500 million years. Concentrating on their transformative variations and hereditary variety adds to how we might interpret life's ingenuity and transformation to changing conditions throughout land time scales

8. Space Investigation

- Tardigrades have been engaged with tests directed in space, presenting them to the unforgiving states of space. These trials assist researchers with understanding the potential for life past Earth and the flexibility of earthbound creatures to

space conditions

CHAPTER THREE

MORPHOLOGY AND BODY DESIGN

The morphology and body design of tardigrades, are unmistakable and adjusted to their minuscule size and different conditions. Here is an outline of their morphology

1. Size and Shape

- Tardigrades are little, going in size from 0.1 to 1.5 millimeters, with most species falling inside the scope of 0.3 to 0.5 millimeters.

- They have an unmistakable barrel-formed body, frequently divided into a few segments

2. Cuticle

- The external layer of the tardigrade is covered by a fingernail skin, a defensive exoskeleton-like construction that gives a protection from ecological circumstances. The fingernail skin is intermittently shed as the tardigrade develops

3. Legs

• Tardigrades have four sets of squat legs, each completion with paws or pull cups, contingent upon the species. The legs are jointed and consider slow, blundering developments

4. Head and Mouthparts:

• The foremost finish of the tardigrade contains the head, which frequently includes tangible extremities. Tardigrades have a buccopharyngeal contraption with stylets or penetrating mouthparts utilized for taking care of

5. Body Division

- The body is divided into locales, with each section relating to a couple of legs. The quantity of fragments can change among species

6. Muscles and Motion

- Tardigrades have longitudinal and roundabout muscles that empower them to contract and broaden their bodies, working with slow slithering developments. They are not known for quick or spry movement

7. Eyespots

- A few types of tardigrades have eyespots, which are straightforward photoreceptor structures that can recognize light yet don't frame pictures. The presence and intricacy of eyespots can shift among species

8. Digestive Framework

- Tardigrades have a basic stomach related framework. The buccopharyngeal contraption prompts a straight stomach that goes through the body. Supplements are ingested through the stomach lining

9. Reproductive Organs

- Tardigrades display sexual proliferation with independent genders. The regenerative organs incorporate testicles in guys and ovaries in females. A few animal groups can likewise duplicate agamically through parthenogenesis

10. Cryptobiosis Designs

- In their cryptobiotic state, tardigrades go through changes at the cell level. They withdraw their legs and head, shaping a got dried out, contracted structure. This state permits them to endure outrageous circumstances

UNIQUE ADAPTATIONS AND FEATURES

Tardigrades, have a few novel variations and highlights that add to their wonderful versatility and endurance in different conditions. Here are a portion of their particular qualities

1. Cryptobiosis

- One of the most exceptional highlights of tardigrades is their capacity to enter a condition of cryptobiosis. In this state, they can endure outrageous circumstances like drying up, freezing, and elevated degrees of radiation by dialing back their digestion to a practically complete stop

2. Anhydrobiosis

- Tardigrades can persevere through outrageous drying out through a cycle called anhydrobiosis.

They can lose practically all of their body water and enter a parched state, really closing down their digestion. When rehydrated, they can continue ordinary exercises

3. Tun Development

• In light of cruel natural circumstances, tardigrades can go through a cycle called tun development. They withdraw their legs and head, framing a dried out, barrel-molded structure that improves their protection from stress

4. Extreme Temperature Resilience

• Tardigrades can get through many temperatures, from close to outright zero (- 273.15°C) to over the limit of water (100°C). A few animal groups have been found in conditions with temperatures surpassing 150°C

5. Resistance to Radiation

- Tardigrades show a prominent protection from ionizing radiation. Studies have demonstrated the way that they can endure portions of radiation many times higher than whatever would be deadly to most different creatures

6. Survival in Space

- Tardigrades have been engaged with tests where they were presented to the vacuum of room and infinite radiation. They showed the capacity to make due and duplicate subsequent to getting back to Earth, featuring their strength in extraterrestrial circumstances

7. Flexible Digestion

- Tardigrades can change their metabolic rate in view of natural circumstances. During times of pressure or negative circumstances, they can dial back their digestion to monitor energy

8. Genomic Versatility

- Tardigrade genomes show proof of flat quality exchange, which permits them to gain qualities from different creatures. This genomic versatility might add to their capacity to adjust to assorted conditions

9. Limited Tactile Organs

- Tardigrades normally have basic tactile organs, for certain species having eyespots that can recognize light. While their tangible capacities are restricted, they are appropriate for their little size and generally stationary way of life

10. Adaptations for Life in Microenvironments

- Tardigrades are much of the time found in microenvironments like greeneries, lichens, and leaf litter, where they can explore through the water film encompassing individual cells

CHAPTER FOUR

REPRODUCTIVE SYSTEM

The conceptive arrangement of tardigrades, otherwise called water bears, shows fascinating attributes, incorporating sexual multiplication with discrete genders and, now and again, abiogenetic proliferation through parthenogenesis. Here is an outline of the conceptive arrangement of tardigrades

1. Sexual Proliferation

• Tardigrades regularly replicate physically, with particular male and female people.

• Guys and females can be separated in view of morphological elements, including the presence of regenerative organs

2. Male Conceptive Framework

- The male conceptive framework comprises of testicles, which produce sperm cells (spermatozoa).

- During mating, guys move sperm to the female for treatment

3. Female Conceptive Framework

- The female conceptive framework incorporates matched ovaries, where eggs (oocytes) are delivered.

- Treatment happens inside, and the female stores the sperm until conditions are reasonable for laying eggs.

4. Egg Laying

- After treatment, the female lays eggs, which are kept in the climate. The particular strategy for egg affidavit can differ among species.

- The eggs are in many cases encased in a defensive construction, like a thick lattice, to protect them from natural dangers

5. Development

- The eggs go through undeveloped turn of events, ultimately incubating into adolescent tardigrades.

- The adolescents look like small renditions of the grown-ups and go through shedding stages as they develop

6. Parthenogenesis (Agamic Generation)

- In certain cases, tardigrades are fit for agamic proliferation through parthenogenesis. Parthenogenesis permits females to deliver posterity without the requirement for preparation.

- This cycle includes the improvement of an unfertilized egg into a feasible posterity

7. Variation in Regenerative Modes

- The capacity to recreate both physically and agamically furnishes tardigrades with adaptability in their regenerative methodologies, possibly permitting them to adjust to shifting natural circumstances

8. Reproductive Procedures in Cruel Conditions

- Tardigrades are known for their capacity to make due in outrageous circumstances. Their regenerative procedures, including the capacity to enter cryptobiosis and endure drying up, add to their general versatility

CHAPTER FIVE
TERRESTIAL ENVIRONMENT

Tardigrades, or water bears, are known to occupy various earthly conditions, exhibiting their versatility to various circumstances ashore. Here are a few earthly conditions where tardigrades are ordinarily found

1. Mosses and Lichens

• Tardigrades are as often as possible related with greeneries and lichens. These microhabitats give a clammy climate, permitting water bears to flourish in the water films encompassing the plant cells

2. Leaf Litter

• Tardigrades are many times found in the leaf litter on woodland floors. The layers of disintegrating leaves make a microenvironment with adequate dampness for water bears to possess

3. Soil

• Tardigrades can be tracked down in different kinds of soil, where they explore through the water films encompassing soil particles. Soil-abiding tardigrades assume fundamental parts in supplement cycling and add to the general biodiversity of soil environments

4. Tree Bark

• Some tardigrade species occupy the bark of trees, especially in the cleft where dampness is held. The bark gives a substrate to them to move and take care of

5. Litter and Humus

• Tardigrades are many times seen as in natural matter like litter and humus. These materials add to the accessibility of water and microorganisms, making reasonable circumstances for water bears

6. Moss Pads

• Tardigrades can be bountiful in greenery pads, where the dampness content is generally high. Greenery pads make microenvironments that offer security and assets for these minute creatures

7. Alpine and Polar Locales

• Tardigrades have been found in outrageous conditions like snow capped and polar locales, where they can get through cruel circumstances, including low temperatures and drying up

8. Cryptobiotic States

• Tardigrades can enter cryptobiotic states in light of ominous circumstances. This capacity permits them to get by in earthly conditions in any event, while confronting parching, outrageous temperatures, or different stressors

9. Urban Conditions

- Tardigrades have been tracked down in metropolitan conditions, including parks, gardens, and, surprisingly, on structures. They can adjust to human-changed scenes as long as reasonable microenvironments with adequate dampness are available

10. Diverse Microhabitats

- Tardigrades can take advantage of an extensive variety of microhabitats inside earthly conditions. They might occupy regions with high moistness, including cleft, interstitial spaces, and surfaces where water is accessible

AQUATIC ENVIRONMENT OF TARDIGRADE

Tardigrade or moss piglet, is found in a variety of bodies of water, demonstrating its adaptability to life in water. Here are some of the aquatic habitats where tardigrades are commonly found

1. Freshwater Habitats

• Tardigrades are commonly found in freshwater environments such as ponds, lakes, rivers, streams, and freshwater moss. Tardigrades live in the water layers associated with these environments, move around, and feed on microorganisms.

2. Marine Habitat

• Some tardigrade species are adapted to marine environments such as coastal areas, intertidal zones, and deeper marine sediments.

They move in a film of water that surrounds the marine substrate.

3. Coastal Areas

• Tardigrades can live in coastal areas of bodies of water and stay very close to the water's edge. Coastal environments represent a dynamic interface between land and water, and tardigrades are found in moist habitats associated with these zones.

4. Algal Mats

• Tardigrades are often associated with algal mats and biofilms in aquatic environments. The algae provide a food source and the tardigrades move in the water film surrounding these mats.

5. Sediments

• Tardigrades are found in bottom sediments of freshwater and marine environments. They move through the spaces between sediment particles and take advantage of the water films present in the spaces

6. Mosses and Bryophytes in Aquatic Environments

• Tardigrades are known to live both in water and in aquatic mosses and bryophytes. These plants provide the tardigrades with substrate to move and eat while also providing access to water.

7. Temporary bodies of water

• Tardigrades can be found in temporary bodies of water such as puddles, rain-filled containers, and seasonal ponds. They are adapted to survive in environments that are regularly dry and rehydrated.

8. Glacial Habitat

• Some tardigrade species are found in glacial habitats where they can tolerate the low temperatures associated with ice and meltwater. Glacial environments pose unique challenges for survival

9. Hot Springs and Hot Springs Pools

• Tardigrades are found in extreme environments such as hot springs and hot spring pools. Some species have adaptations that allow them to survive at high temperatures

10. Hydrothermal Vents

• Tardigrades are less common, but they are found in hydrothermal vent ecosystems on the ocean floor. These environments are characterized by high pressure, extreme temperatures, and mineral-rich water.

EXTREMOPHILIC HABITAT

An extremophile habitat is an environment characterized by extreme conditions such as high or low temperatures, high salinity, high pressure, acidity, alkalinity, or radiation levels. Tardigrades, also known as tardigrades or moss piglets, are known for their remarkable ability to survive in a variety of extremophile habitats. Below are examples of extremophile habitats where tardigrades have been found.

1. Polar Regions

- Tardigrades live in polar regions such as the North Pole and the South Pole. Tardigrades can survive in the extreme cold and harsh conditions of these environments and are commonly found in mosses, lichens, and soil

2. Desert

- Tardigrades can survive extreme dryness and high daytime temperatures. Found in desert environments where Common in desert soils, mosses, and lichens

3. Hot Springs and Geothermal Areas

• Some species of tardigrades breed in hot springs and geothermal areas where they can tolerate high temperatures and extreme fluctuations. Tardigrades are commonly found in surrounding sediments and biofilms

4. Deep Sea Hydrothermal Vents

• Tardigrades are found in deep sea hydrothermal vents where they are exposed to high temperatures, pressure, and chemical toxicity. They live in the sediments and biofilms surrounding these springs

5. Oxygen-deficient environments

• Tardigrades can survive in environments with low oxygen levels, such as anaerobic sediments and environments with high concentrations of hydrogen sulfide

6. High-altitude environments

- Some tardigrade species live in environments such as mountain peaks and alpine areas. Some live in highland environments. . They can tolerate the cold and low oxygen levels associated with high altitudes.

7. Nuclear Contamination Sites

- Tardigrades have been shown to be resistant to ionizing radiation and able to survive in highly radioactive contaminated environments, such as pH environments. Found in environments with pH levels. Can withstand a wide range of pH levels

8. Extreme pH Environments

- Tardigrades have been found in situations with extraordinary pH levels, counting acidic and soluble situations. They can endure a wide run of pH conditions

9. Space

- Tardigrades have been uncovered to the vacuum of space and enormous radiation in tests conducted on space missions. They have demonstrated the ability to outlive within the extraordinary conditions of external space

10. Underground Caves

- Tardigrades have been found in underground caves, where they can survive in moo supplement situations and fluctuating temperature

CHAPTER SIX

TARDIGRADE ECOLOGY AND BEHAVIOR

NOURISHING PROPENSITIES AND DIET

tardigrades, in spite of their modest estimate, play vital parts in their environments as microphagous buyers. Their nourishing propensities and count calories are moderately straightforward however basic for supplement cycling and vitality exchange inside different environments. Here's an outline of the nourishing propensities and count calories of tardigrades

1. Microphagous Feeding

• Tardigrades are microphagous living beings, meaning they nourish on little particles and microorganisms. They basically expend liquids extricated from plant cells, green growth, microbes, organisms, and other infinitesimal living beings display in their environment

2. Buccopharyngeal Apparatus

- Tardigrades have a buccopharyngeal device, which is basically a mouth encompassed by a ring of stylets or puncturing mouthparts. These stylets are utilized to cut plant cells, algal cells, or the bodies of other tiny living beings to extricate fluids

3. Feeding Process

- When a tardigrade experiences appropriate nourishment sources in its environment, it amplifies its stylets and pierces the cell dividers or layers of the prey. It at that point sucks out the substance, counting cytoplasm and other cellular liquids, employing a combination of solid withdrawals and suction

4. Filter Feeding

• Some tardigrade species lock in in channel bolstering, where they inactively collect particles suspended within the surrounding water column. They may use cilia or other structures to direct water flow and capture small particles, such as bacteria and algae, for consumption

5. Feeding Inclinations:

• Tardigrades are sharp feeders, equipped for eating an extensive variety of food sources relying upon accessibility. Nonetheless, they will generally favor gentler plant tissues, green growth, and microorganisms, which are more straightforward to puncture and concentrate liquids from.

6. Digestion and Supplement Ingestion:

• When consumed, the extricated liquids are processed inside the tardigrade's stomach related framework. Supplements, including sugars, proteins, and other natural particles, are retained through the stomach lining and used for energy, development, and generation.

7. Frequency of Taking care of:

• Tardigrades have somewhat sluggish metabolic rates and can make due for broadened periods without food. They might enter times of torpidity or cryptobiosis when food is scant, preserving energy until appropriate taking care of chances emerge.

8. Role in Biological systems:

- Regardless of their little size, tardigrades assume significant parts in their biological systems as purchasers and supplement recyclers. By benefiting from microorganisms and partaking in disintegration processes, they add to supplement cycling and energy stream inside earthbound and amphibian natural surroundings

DEVELOPMENT AND HEADWAY

Tardigrades, otherwise called water bears or greenery piglets, show interesting and captivating headway notwithstanding their little size and somewhat straightforward body structure. Here is an outline of tardigrade development and velocity:

1. Slow and Intentional Development:

- Tardigrades move gradually and intentionally, commonly at

speeds going from a couple of micrometers to a couple of millimeters each second. Their developments are somewhat lazy contrasted with numerous different microorganisms.

2. Legged Velocity:

• Tardigrades have four sets of squat legs, each completion with hooks or attractions cups. These legs are jointed and empower tardigrades to creep and explore through their current circumstance.

3. Muscular Compressions:

• Tardigrades utilize strong constrictions to expand and withdraw their legs, working with development. They depend on longitudinal and round muscles to create the important powers for velocity.

4. Adhesive Cushions and Hooks:

- The legs of tardigrades are furnished with glue cushions or paws that assist them with holding onto surfaces. These designs give footing and dependability as tardigrades get across various substrates.

5. Lumbering Stride:

- Tardigrades show a stumbling stride portrayed by sluggish, musical developments of their legs. They move in a planned way, switching back and forth among expanding and withdrawing their legs as they creep.

6. Hydrostatic Skeleton:

- Tardigrades have a hydrostatic skeleton, which comprises of liquid filled compartments that offer help and empower development. Changes in strain inside the body permit them to broaden and withdraw their legs.

7. Navigational Way of behaving:

- Tardigrades display fundamental navigational way of behaving, answering natural signs like light and compound slopes. They might adjust their bearing of development because of upgrades from their environmental elements.

8. Swimming and Drifting:

- Some tardigrade species are fit for swimming or drifting in water, utilizing their legs to move themselves through the water segment. They may likewise use air bubbles caught on their bodies to increment lightness.

9. Response to Ecological Circumstances:

- Tardigrades can change their headway because of changes in natural circumstances, like temperature, moistness, and substrate surface. They might turn out to be more dynamic or enter cryptobiosis to endure troublesome circumstances.

10. Limited Hopping skill:

- While tardigrades essentially slither and walk, a few animal groups have been seen to take little leaps by broadening their legs powerfully. Be that as it may, their ability to bounce is moderately restricted contrasted with different microorganisms

Printed in Great Britain
by Amazon